THE TAME MAGPIE

ALSO BY PAUL VIOLI

Poetry

She'll Be Riding Six White Horses
Automatic Transmissions
Waterworks
In Baltic Circles
Harmatan
Some Poems
Splurge
Likewise
The Curious Builder
The Anamorphosis
Fracas
Breakers
Overnight

Prose

Selected Accidents, Pointless Anecdotes

THE TAME MAGPIE

New Poems
By Paul Violi

Hanging Loose Press
Brooklyn, New York

Published by Hanging Loose Press, 231 Wyckoff Street, Brooklyn, New York 11217-2208. All rights reserved. No part of this book may be reproduced without the publisher's written permission, except for brief quotations in reviews.

www.hangingloosepress.com

Printed in the United States of America
10 9 8 7 6 5 4 3 2 1

Cover art: Alessandro Magnasco (c.1667-1749), *The Tame Magpie*. Oil on canvas, 25 x 29 1/2 in. (63.5 x 74.9 cm). Purchase, Katherine D. W. Glover Gift, 1984 (1984.191). Location: The Metropolitan Museum of Art, New York, NY, USA. Photo Credit: Image copyright © The Metropolitan Museum of Art. Image source: Art Resource, NY.

Cover design: Marie Carter

ISBN 978-1-934909-40-9

Library of Congress cataloging-in-publication available on request.

The last poem in this book appeared in *Hanging Loose*. Unfortunately, we have no way of knowing if any of the other poems appeared in magazines. If they did, we regret that we can't acknowledge the publications by name, but we offer our thanks on Paul Violi's behalf.

CONTENTS

INTRODUCTION

1

Paul Violi, as vigorous as anyone we knew, died of cancer at 66 in April of 2011, leaving a workroom crammed with files, binders, poems in various stages, letters, notebooks, magazines, books—a writer's rich disarray. When Ann, Paul's wife, began to sort through his papers, she came upon some new poems (written since the publication of *Overnight*, in 2007) and wondered what we thought about them. There were 60 or so pages in Paul's usual single-spacing, mostly what looked liked finished, uncollected poems but also notes, poem starts, versions of the same poem, etc. Some of the apparently finished works looked familiar, though there was no indication which poems if any had already been published (with the exception mentioned below). Nor did the pages appear to be in any real order, though the very last—and the last piece in this book—was his funny and moving poem dedicated to his friend Bob Hershon, which we knew had been published in *Hanging Loose* magazine (and later reprinted in *Best American Poetry*). We saw pretty quickly that there was enough material for a new book, one which Paul would have been proud of. After a few tries at a title, it hit us just about simultaneously that "The Tame Magpie" was not only a quintessential Violi poem; it was a Violi title, as well as the poem most appropriate to kick off a Violi book.

2

Paul grew up on the North Shore of Long Island, as did Ann; both spent a lot of time in and near the water. He studied English literature and art history at Boston University. After some time spent in the Peace Corps in Nigeria and some traveling in Africa and Asia on his own, he returned to the U.S., living in New York City and working for WCBS-TV and, in the early 1970s, as Managing Editor of *Architectural Forum*. He took an active part in the community of poets centered around The Poetry Project, in downtown Manhattan, and for several months at the end of 1977 was the Project's Interim Director. He also chaired the Museum of Modern Art Associate Council Poetry Committee and had a hand in the MoMA poetry series sponsored by the Kulchur Foundation. For the last three decades of his life, Paul was a busy and very popular college teacher. At the time of the onset of his illness he was teaching in the graduate writing program at The New School and in the Department of English and Comparative Literature at Columbia University, where he had taken over courses taught for years by Kenneth Koch, who was a great admirer of Paul's work.

Almost from the time of our meeting in 1970, the three of us got together regularly for coffee or drinks in SoHo (where we joked, gossiped, vented, and talked at least a little shop), and we remained close for forty years. Our poems didn't look or feel similar, but we were on the same wave-length about almost everything to do with poetry. Like us, Paul came to be associated with the so-called Second Generation New York School. Whether he truly belongs in this category is another story; he himself always had mixed feelings about it. Pound, for example, was as important to him as the French modernists; so were Coleridge and Keats.

Although Paul's poems became stronger, and more resonant, in the ensuing decades, what is most striking about them was present right from the start: his sharp wit and humor, his satirical spirit, his formal inventiveness, his frequent lyric impulse. His masterful, riddling dramatic monologues (with personae including, among many others, Homer, Lao-Tze, Custer, Fragonard, and a lappet-winged vulture), which made their bow in *Overnight* under the title "I.D." and are continued here, demonstrate all these qualities. Comic lists drawn from everyday life were a Violi specialty: a TV schedule, the call of a horse race, a "Police Blotter," an index to an imaginary book. A wonderful reader, Paul drew big crowds, reducing just about everyone, including us, to helpless laughter.

Although he was best known for his humorous and satirical poems—among the latter is "King Nasty," his devastating satire on the subject of the French Revolution's Reign of Terror—he wrote deft love poems too, and lyric poems about the natural world. His experience in Africa produced his incisive, sharply detailed, book-length poem "Harmatan." He was always reading history, and anecdotes from his reading made it into any number of his poems. Paul won his fair share of poetry awards, but it's hard not to feel that his comic gift was ultimately double-edged. Comic poets have always had trouble being taken seriously in America, and, as talented as Paul was, in the eyes of many his reputation remains less than it should be. However, to those who really know his work, he is up there with America's best.

Charles North and Tony Towle
December 2013

Note: Early in 1970, Paul Violi and Charles North attended Tony Towle's poetry workshop at The Poetry Project; their association began from that point.

THE TAME MAGPIE

THE TAME MAGPIE

(*Allessandro Magnasco, c.1677-1749*)

"An assortment of people from the fringes
of society have gathered to watch
the spectacle of a man trying to teach
a magpie how to sing—an impossible task!"

Impossible, yes, if the stragglers
At the Met today don't turn off
Their trilling cells for a minute and stand
Where Magnasco forces them to stand,
On the fringe of the fringes of society.
But consider The Contumacious Kid.
He squirms up next to the museum guide
Squinting at Magnasco's quick brushwork
For details that defy the obvious
And—behold! It's Ambrose Bierce—
Who for his first day on the job
Sports the uniform of Paraguay's
Most optimistic admiral.
"Enlighten me, Admiral Bierce!"
Together they scan the squalor and decay,
The rotten gate, the ruined arches
Of a botched civilization, and berate
The ungrateful layabouts
On the dilapidated dock.
"That gangly man," says Bierce,
"Is he beseeching or conducting the bird?
Of art, who is hungrier,
He or that swollen magpie?
The sloucher in the Chico Marx hat,
The Minerva lookalike,
The drunken soldier, the mother
Holding forth her infant

For a baptism of folly—
The entire scene impels me to say,
O despondent youth,
Consider your little sisters,
Behold the fowls of the air:
Are they not flammable?
Are ye not much better than they?
Why take ye thought for raiment?
I say unto you, Kiddo,
That even Solomon in all his glory
Was not arrayed like one of these.
Adversity? Doubt? Dismay?
Consider the goldfinch who feeds on thorn
And thistle yet sings a lovely song.
That magpie perched atop a stack
Of wine casks like a short wick, a black flame
On a fat candle, is singing, damn it!
That low smudge of sunlight a foil or halo
Behind him, lets your eyes grow sharp
To what (as some sages sing)
A black flame can illuminate.
That teacher has been knocked back
On his butt not by exasperation but
By a miracle of futility.
That thieving pest, head raised, beak open,
Has indeed let a note or two fly.
Besides, Kid, since a magpie can already
Steal like a human, getting it to warble
Like one shouldn't be much of a stretch."

SUBARU
ALL REASONABLE OFFERS CONSIDERED

See yourself cutting and splashing
Over miles of twisting black road
Overrun swept this way and that
In the high and low turns
By the flooded creek
Silver black road and white water intertwined
Like coupling serpents
Writhing in the night storm
Where would you rather be
Than behind the high-beam eyes
Of the car named not after Tiresias
But in honor of Atlas
And his five starry daughters
Mythic thrills you will enjoy
In the complete safety
Of this Subaru Forester
Silver with black trim
Four wheel drive 35+K
30 mpg
AC CD
New tires
All reasonable offers considered

FROM THE GREEK ANTHOLOGY

II after Asclepiades

Sweet the snow brought down to fieldhands on a summer day,
And sweet the sight of the spring bloom to sailors
Drifting into port from a rough winter.
But the sweetest thing is when one blanket covers
Two lovers who can tell the same story
Of how they got under it.

III after Asclepiades

What is sweeter than love?
Every other delight is a distant second,
Too distant to compare.
Yes, I even spit honey off my lips.
But if you don't know this, you can't
Tell one rose from another.

VII after Meleager

Let's take some wild risks, light the lights, I'm on my way!
Courage and wine have a purpose in life—revelry.
Reason's a straggler, not made to follow a quick heart,
Soon staggering far behind, soon forgotten.
And Philosophy takes years to construct, a sea-wall
Built block upon block, hand over hand,
Year after year only to be
Demolished by one wave.
That's all I know—the same wave
That washed away even the mind of Zeus.

VIII   after Rufinus

Mortal me vs. immortal Love,
One on one it's an even fight.
But against Love and Wine
I'd bet against myself.

XI   after Meleager

Again Love pounces on me like an eagle.
Again it's too weak afterwards
To lift its wings, to fly off and leave me be.

XIII   after Meleager

Cupid: God of love, sex, pleasure, etc.
Abode: Mount Olympus.
Symbol: Bow, hearts, lamps, kisses and wings.
Consort: Psyche.
Children: Voluptas.
M.O.: Gold or lead arrowheads, nothing but trouble.
Parentage: Problematic, Love and War by default
Since not earth, nor heaven nor the sea
Have claimed him as their own.
The little bastard!

XV   after Paulus Silentiarius

A man bitten by a rabid dog
Thereafter finds the beast's reflection
In every lovely pool.
But what has me by the throat
So whether looking in the sea waves
In a whirling river or in a cup of wine
I'm looking at you?

XX   after Meleager

Leave her alone, Mosquitoes,
Attack me instead.
Let her sleep, shrill blood-suckers
  Wanting to feast or nestle
On her soft arms.
    I can't blame you but I'll crush you.

XXXIII   after Meleager

Take this message to her, Dorcas,
Then just to be sure she gets it take it again.
Take it three times, as fast as a gazelle.
Fly like a gazelle—but wait a second!
I'm not finished—No, go ahead
Before I start babbling like a fool.
Don't say anything except—No
Say everything!
Where's your hat what's your hurry?
Hold it—I'll go myself.
No, wait, we'll both go.

BLAGUE

For CN

This French joke that I first heard decades ago?

> First Frenchman: *How are you?*

> Second Frenchman: *My mother died today.*

> First Frenchman: *Hmmm . . . At what time?*

> Second Frenchman: *10 o'clock.*

> First Frenchman: *Hmmm . . . 10 o'clock . . .*

Well, I told it to a guy yesterday
And today he told me he told it
To a couple of Frenchmen.

They wanted to know what time it was
When I told it to him.

I told all this to Michael and Tony at Café Loup tonight
And they asked what time it was
When the guy told me what the Frenchmen said.

I'm still not sure I get it.

PEIRE VIDAL

I nudge—clutch something cold
And heavy under the pillow,
Then hold it—a chrome-plated pistol—
Up to the moonglow.

"Robbers have you worried?"
"No," she said, "I'm married."

FURTHER I.D.'S

I

I was the first to write in that willful
And various style the Greeks had no name for.
Perseus considered my enemies victims
And said that I broke my jaw-tooth on them.
My friend Horace said I grind out
Indistinguishable poems
And called them bratverse.
He complained I wrote so much
My funeral pyre would need
No other fuel than my own books.
To hell with his pesky notions of perfection:
As some sages sing
It's the impurities that give color to the flames.
Of one of my poems only one word
Remains: Vulture.
Though little survives of the others
But phrases and flotsam, I am as I was,
Loving crowds and solitude, with the shoreline
My sometime refuge from them and myself,
Wind at my back, sand as fine
As powder, as wispy as smoke
Blown across the glowing hardpack,
Big-eyed skittish creatures, oddities,
Little beauties and what-not
Shadowed by scavengers,
The chance a surprise or two
Will ignite an idle hour.

Who am I?

II

Plato and Aristotle argued over this and that,
Over something from nothing,
And over what made me laugh.
In childhood I retreated to a garden shed
Where I wrote and studied so devotedly
My indulgent, gentle father, to remind me
Of neglected chores, tied an ox to my door.
Three days passed before I noticed the beast.
To prevent another beast, money,
From distracting me, I gave most of mine
To charity then squandered the rest.
I went to Athens but told no one there my name,
Not even Aristotle, for why should I have
A little renown bestowed on me
From merely visiting a famous place?
Better to have my visit give a place
Something to brag about.
I titled my first book *The Little World*
And right before I died at 109
Published my last, *The Great World*.
Plato wished to burn every copy he could find.
Nothing exists but atoms and empty space;
All the rest is rumor and guesswork.
(Poetry is worthless.)
Meanwhile, entangled, awhirl or dancing freely
In the vastness of such a hive, try to remain fearless.
Aristotle said my laugh was an echo
Of the highest ethical good: Cheerfulness.
But Seneca thought it contemptuous, citing reports
That I would laugh at strangers in the street,
And the fact that, Abdera being my hometown,
A nasty cackle was called Abderian Laughter.
Couldn't they hear it all together, a chorus of one?
Kindly mirth, empathy, reckless sympathy, scorn,
All in the same raw ardent voice,

Cockerel or rooster—young or ancient,
Ancient and eager in the dawn.

Who am I?

III

Three explanations circulated amongst the people
As to why on the opening night of my play
The theater roof collapsed:
I. The rafters were rotten.
II. The gods had passed judgment on a bad play.
III. The gods were jealous of its greatness.
Though obviously the best, the third
Explanation was not entirely correct.
I waited until speculation peaked
Before pronouncing the real reason:
The gods knew a finer play
Would never be performed there
And thus deemed the theatre obsolete.
I was popular.
I improved the lot of the poor.
I was accused of killing my mother.
I had a big belly and skinny legs.
To restore morale after Rome burned
I invited thousands to a party in my private gardens.
All feasted on my generosity, all admitted
To being overawed by my musical compositions,
And all agreed that the torchlight—torches
I myself designed, each one containing
A bundled living Christian—made the night
As bright as daytime in August.

Who am I?

IV

I built this house so the stairway expands
As it rises above the sea, not to a front door
But directly to the roof: rectangular, red,
Flat to its rail-less edge, a runway
Below the infinite night where on occasion
I like to dance with extremes balanced
In my outstretched arms, in my open hands.
Critics describe my writing as surreal.
After the Eastern Front, Surrealism was child's play.
I wrote a novel—sad, wry, horrible, subtle, brutal—
That was a string of vignettes, portraits
Of desperate cosmopolites and grim commoners,
An elegant necklace slowly tightened into a garrote.
Soldiers whose eyelids had frozen and broken off,
They don't mean to be rude,
Forever staring back at the reader.
When Naples was liberated, the doors
Of the asylum thrown open, the lunatics
Ran joyously through the streets, down to the bay,
And then, like Europe, didn't know what to do,
And stared at each other in a wild despair.
The Tatars thought of war as the dead killing the living
And to savor that irony liked to tie a prisoner
To a corpse that would rot and slowly kill him.
When the Finns trapped a Russian army,
Surrounding it in a forest with a ring of fire,
Herds of terrified horses leapt out of the flames
Only to land in the river the minute a 30-below wind
Arrived and froze it and them immediately.
They're still there months later, mile
After mile, horseheads protruding through the ice,
Necks stretched back toward the charred shore,
Horseheads about the height of a bar stool
On which I sit and smoke and talk to you.
A mishandled corkscrew and from one of my cold
Numb fingers a drop of blood seems to have fallen

Into a glass of white wine . . . or ice water.
It dissolves in undulant swirls and disappears.
I wonder how far I can follow where
The invisible dancer behind those veils is leading me.
On my deathbed, perplexing a few witnesses,
I embraced Catholicism and Mao's communism.

Who am I?

V

I introduced Swinburne to cognac.
He told me the Goncourt brothers dropped by
Unannounced one day to find him in his study
Reciting Aeschylus in the original
To a severed hand he held before him.
He kept it for that sole purpose, enticing his muse,
In a jar of formaldehyde on his desk.
They fled without saying a word.
Attacked on a beach in Somalia, I fled,
Swimming with a spear through my face
Back to the ship where my rescuers
Hauled me aboard by the shaft.
From time to time I drank to excess.
Mint-juleps, Brandy-smashes, Whiskeys,
Gin-slings, Cock-tail sherry, Cobblers,
Rum-salads, Streaks of Lightning,
Morning Glories: I drank myself through America.
Many found my respect for Mormonism
As disagreeable as my admiration for Islam.
I mastered 29 languages,
Each increasing the force of the cascade
Under which I held my crystal glass.
Soldier, spy, explorer, anthropologist,
Historian, pilgrim, poet, sexologist:
Because of my service to the Crown
I expected a diplomatic post.
My antagonists saw to it that I was sent
To the Bight of Benin, a miasmic,
Fever-ridden deathtrap where I found
It easy to despise all races equally.
One king crucified a fellow in honor of my visit.
I almost went mad and begged to be recalled.
In my three years there I wrote only nine books.
When I died my wife, my dear, darling Isabelle,
That glorious auburn-haired woman, burned
My diaries, journals, papers, though she resisted

Consigning to the flames one work of erotica
Until my ghost commanded her to do so,
And then only on its third appearance.

Who am I?

VI

I preached to large congregations.
I published theological treatises.
Scripture was always on my lips
But those who did business with me
Soon found I was a mere swindler.
At length I turned my attention from
Theology to the worst part of politics.
I belonged to that class whose office it is
To render in troubled times to exasperated parties
Those services from which honest men
Shrink in dusgust and prudent men
In fear, the class of fanatical knaves.
Violent, malignant, heedless of truth,
Insensible to shame, insatiable of notoriety,
Delighting in intrigue, in tumult,
In mischief for its own sake, I toiled
For years in the darkest mines of faction.
I lived among libelers and false witnesses.
I was the keeper of a secret purse from which agents
Too vile to be acknowledged received hire,
And the director of a secret press whence pamphlets,
Bearing no name, were daily issued.
In this way of life, I assumed more names
Than the devil himself, and at one time
Flitted among four different lodgings
In the malebolge of London.
When my conspiracies were detected
And my associates were in dismay,
I laughed and bid them farewell,
And told them they were novices,
That I had been used to flight,
Concealment and disguise, and that I
Should never leave off plotting while I lived.

Who am I?

27

VII

I do not see very well in the dark.
I have a bald red head.
I like to sunbathe,
And while I do I defecate on my feet
To keep them cool and clean.
I am attracted to rubber and plastic
Which I like to rip off your house and car.
If you bother me I will hiss at you,
If you threaten, I will vomit on you.
Caveat Lector: I can with stunning accuracy
Spew a good ten feet.
My Latin name, *Cathartes Aura*,
Means cleansing breeze.

Who am I?

VIII

Why was I known as the King of Peace?
I was a tightwad.
I mired my court in squalor while pouring money
Into my prize accomplishment: a brigade of giants.
My ragtag, penurious diplomats
Scoured Europe for recruits.
My ambassador to London received a bounty
Of 1300 pounds sterling
For finding a 7' Irishman.
I gazed upon that brigade like a boy
Cherishing his collection of toy soldiers.
Since I would never risk them harm in battle,
I, of course, avoided wars.
Atheists, Catholics, Calvinists, Philosophers:
They were all the same to me: laughable.
I lived under a cloud of tobacco smoke
And malevolent rage.
If I met a lady on the street, I'd give her
A good kick and send her home to her brats.
If I met a clergyman, I'd cane him.
I loved Swedish beer, hunted wild boar
And slaughtered partridge by the thousands.
I despised literature.
I don't know whom I detested more,
My daughter or my insolent, Francophile son.
He asked too many questions.
I woke him up each morning with a cannon blast.
I threw dinner plates at him
And forced him to eat putrid food.
I broke his flute over his head.
I tried to strangle him with a curtain cord
And dumped him in a dungeon.
He grew up to become a military genius
But was accused of depravity
And perversion so abhorrent
They would make a satirist blanch.

Who am I?

IX

"The Humors of Cremation," a double-spread
Making fun of that new fashion
For the disposal of the deceased,
Was the first of my vignette cartoons.
They became a *Puck* mainstay,
With Grant my favorite target.
Ambrose Bierce said that as a printmaker
I was a giant with a pencil
But called the poet with whom I collaborated
A pygmy, a fat-witted fool whose words
Made weak the pictures I made so strong.
Bunner was his name.
But I liked the man's style.
He deliberately kept it plain and simple
So anyone could understand the cartoons,
Particularly the odious and greedy.

Who am I?

X

I survived two shipwrecks in one day.
Rebuked for the way I waged war, I replied:
War is cruelty; you can not refine it.
And the crueler it is, the shorter it is;
And the shorter it is, the less time politicians,
Preachers and reporters have to interfere with it.
Truth, like gunpowder and religion,
Should be dispensed in careful measures.
My men swore the best powder consisted
Of just the right ratio of cow manure
To a drunken bishop's piss.
My bummers destroyed the great houses
And affectionately labeled the chimneys
That stood in the ashes monuments to me.
I believe nothing is more thrilling—
Nothing can compare in intensity
To maintaining in the mayhem of battle
A cold and utter decisiveness.
But a shoddy performance of *Hamlet*
Flustered—enraged me to such a degree that
Though sitting with other generals in the balcony
I yelled my contempt down to the stage.
A discomfited Grant insisted I leave the theatre.
The newspapers that called him a drunkard
And accused him of every sin
In the calendar, called me crazy.
Consequently, we both learned
How to be silent in several languages.
The presidency was not for me.
Honor would have been the first casualty.
Besides, my wife would have filled
The White House with priests.

Who am I?

XI

Last in my West Point class, I became the youngest,
Most photographed general in the army.
Sherman, who dressed like a sloppy old farmer,
Said glory in warfare was all moonshine,
But he understood the heart of a cavalryman.
"My steeds were all pawing at the threshold of the morn."
One general I knew always tied the tips
Of his moustaches behind his head before a charge.
Jeb Stuart had half of his snipped off by a bullet.
I wanted to make the enemy taste lightning.
The day I joined my brigade at Gettysburg
I was wearing tight green corduroy trousers,
A black velveteen Hussar jacket
With silver piping on the sleeves,
A sailor's shirt with silver stars on the collar,
A red cravat, gleaming jackboots
And a wide-brimmed hat.
Before I slept at night I sprinkled cinnamon oil
On my long, glistening ringlets and curled
Them around candles—a trick my wife taught me.
By the time I was killed on Last Stand Hill,
My hair had thinned and receded so much,
Nobody bothered to take my scalp . . .
Nor my blue shirt, red cravat,
And fringed buckskin jacket.

Who am I?

XII

Truer than truth itself, they said
Of Benedetti's history, how he managed
Simultaneously to praise the victors
And to blow ashes into their eyes.
As he walked the riverbank near Novara
After the slaughter, after rapacious peasants
Had stripped the dead, after days of rain
Had cleansed their drained and gaping wounds
And made them less difficult to examine,
He composed his testament with his doctor's eye.
For him there was no telling French
From Roman, Venetian from Greek,
Only whose courage had made them
Most vulnerable: Those with throat wounds.
I hope some find in my memoir a covenant of sorts:
The solace of unadorned fact.
After the first day at Shiloh the bodies
Of the fallen were so numerous
An observer could walk across the peach orchard
Without stepping on the ground.
I who couldn't stand the sight of blood
Saw the nearby pond stained red,
The corpses covered with blossoms.
Throughout the night rain fell in torrents,
Lightning exposed vultures ripping apart the dead.
I made my headquarters under a tree
A few hundred yards back from the river bank.
My ankle was so much swollen from the fall
Of my horse the Friday night preceding
And the bruise was so painful that I could get no rest.
Some time after midnight, growing restive
Under the storm and the continuous pain,
I moved back to the log house under the bank.
This had been taken as a hospital,
And all night wounded men were being brought in,
Their wounds dressed, a leg or an arm amputated

As the case might require, and everything
Being done to save life or alleviate suffering.
The sight was more unendurable
Than encountering the enemy's fire,
And I returned to my tree in the rain.

Who am I?

XIII

In my boyhood approaching Chartres
In a carriage, I remarked to my father
That the exterior of a Gothic cathedral
Looked like the back of a tapestry.
Asked to be the first professor
Of medieval history at Harvard,
I answered: only if you can't find someone
Who knows the subject better than I do.
When the students asked difficult questions
I was heard to say, How should I know?
Why don't you look it up yourself?
Though in the Middle Ages the ribalds laughed
At notions of infinite love and harmony,
Most students—surrounded by a diorama
Of sorrow, plague, pestilence, famine,
Inundations, cruelty, perversity, stupidity,
Misery without cause and horrors undefined,
Catastrophes world-wide and accidents in corners—
Kept certain questions to themselves.
The return of a female deity, the mother of Christ,
Helped revitalize European civilization
And lead it out of darkened centuries.
I never spoke of my wife's suicide.
Stanny White designed the tomb,
St. Gaudens the bronze figure, unfathomably
Deep and dark, cloaked, looking down
And leaning back resting against the stone.
Do not allow the world to tag this figure with a name!
Every magazine writer wants to label it
As some American patent medicine
For popular consumption—Grief, Despair, Pear's Soap,
Or Macy's Men's Suits Made to Measure.
It was meant to ask a question, not to give an answer;
And the man who answers will be damned
To eternity like the men who answered the Sphinx.

Who am I?

XIV

I formed a regiment that fought at Culloden.
I dunked the greatest political philosopher
Of the age into a tub of ice-cold water.
I helped found England's first home for abandoned children.
I liked to fill my country house, a little Versailles,
With guests and fill their beds with itching powder.
I was a Knight of the Garter, a fellow
Of the Royal Society, and a Grand Master
Of the Premier of the Grand Lodge in London.
I made a bet that I could fill a theatre
By advertising that a performer
Would stuff himself into a quart bottle.
When he failed to appear, the audience,
Which included the king's brother,
Rioted and gutted the place.
My wife and I had six children.
None of my sons survived me,
So my dukedom died with me.
My mother-in-law said that at 52
I had the sense of humor of a pitiless 15-year-old.
I founded a hospital for old cows and knackered horses.
I was most fond of alarmingly ugly lapdogs.
I financed the education of ex-slaves.
I once invited to dinner 18 people,
None of whom knew each other, all of whom stuttered.

Who am I?

XV

I seem to have derived more
Than my talent from my native province,
To have been indebted to it
Also for my breeding and my temperament,
For the graciousness of my destiny,
For my benevolence, for a nature
That was delighted to be alive,
A gaiety which hovered above
The seriousness of life,
A gentle obstinacy in pursuit of success,
A leisured activity, an indolent diligence,
An ambition to gather, in life and in art,
Only the rosebuds,
A love of flowing, effortless existence,
An indifference to the future—
And all this was sustained,
Heightened by a bright trust in Providence,
A confidence which inspired this reply
From me to a question on my beginnings
And development as an artist:
Manage as best you can, said Nature,
And shoved me into existence.

Who am I?

XVI

I was the last of my breed, traveling
From court to court until they
Were all ravaged by Saracens
And abandoned by God.
I tried to teach the kings that hired me
The difference between buffoons and true poets.
I rigged my songs to prevent riffraff
From ruining them, made them so intricate
That if crooners changed one word, form
And sense would collapse at their feet.
I often composed along a riverbank,
Alone and joyful, for songs
That do not spring from joy have no luster.
Here I am again and it's a lovely day.
Blossoms cover the pathways like a snowfall,
Whitecaps jump high and low,
A windburst leaps over the rocky bank
And turns white as it sweeps the blossoms
Off the cherry trees, off the lawn,
Spins them as high as the turkey vultures
Gliding above me, that now look
Like they're drawn into the downdraft,
Now like they're cast out
Of a furious metamorphosis.
Blossoms and vultures wrapped in the same
White whirling minute, until
The birds slide off on ruffled wing
And the blossoms settle in the down-sift
Along with more than a few free
Particles of my own nature, not
Exactly where they were before.

Who am I?

Answer Key

I	Lucilius
II	Democritus
III	Nero Claudius Caesar Augustus Germanicus
IV	Curzio Malaparte
V	Sir Richard Burton
VI	Robert Ferguson
VII	Lappet-Faced Vulture
VIII	Frederick William I
IX	Joseph Keppler
X	William Tecumseh Sherman
XI	George Armstrong Custer
XII	Ulysses S. Grant
XIII	Henry Adams
XIV	John, 2nd Duke of Montague
XV	Fragonard
XVI	Giraut Riquier

SO MUCH DEPENDS

So much depends
On
The white chickens
Martha Stewart
Fluffs
And
Blow-dries
Before
Letting them
Free range
On her front lawn

STALIN AND MAO SCHTICKOMYTHIA

What's what?

What's up?

What's up with you?

What's it look like?

What do you mean?

What do you mean what do I mean?

What's eating you?

What do you care?

What's your problem?

What's it to you?

What are you, a wiseguy?

What if I am?

What if I—

What if you what?

What are you, deaf?

What makes you ask?

What's this all about?

What's in it for me?

Whatever you say.

What a deal.

HEAP

1955 to 57 Russwood
Drugs, Inc. stock clerk; empty
boxes torn-up and piled in the
storeroom at day's end. Newspaper
delivery route (bicycle). Mowed lawns,
mounds of clippings. 1957-58 Russwood Drugs,
lunch counter clerk, neat little heaps of old coffee
grounds dumped in the garbage bin; egg salad, tuna fish,
cold cuts piled in stainless steel racks. 1958-62 Fur trapper
(muskrat mostly, their dens heaps of twigs and sticks, snow
melted on top if occupied; stacks of pelts; trapline extended
from Cold Spring Harbor to Smithtown, Long Island). 1959+
Greenlawn Stationery, lunch counter clerk (a.k.a. soda jerk); sliced
beef heaped in the middle of bread slices to make sandwich appear
generously stuffed). 1959 (?) Sutter's Luncheonette, Greenlawn, L. I.,
heaps of bundled newspapers, sections to be collated on Sunday mornings.
1959 Sold Christmas trees on roadside; pile of unsold fir trees thrown in the
snow. 1960+ Oakwood Construction Company, L.I., laborer; heaps of
blocks, brick, sand, cement. 1960+ Moran Construction laborer; Redsum
Drugs, Syosset Drugstore, clerk. 1960 summer, Cowhey Shipping Supply
Co. Brooklyn, N.Y., chains, portholes, anchors piled in the yard; guard
dogs. 1960-61 DeLuca's Hardware, Greenlawn, clerk, Saturdays; shove a
scoop into a pile of nails, pour them onto the scale pan; stacks of cement
bags, sacks of grass seed, etc. Trash removal, East Northport Town Dump,
vast heaps bulldozers plow under a cloud of gulls and crows. 1960-61
Thomas Cook & Son, NYC, mail dept., canvas mail bags unstrung and
dumped on the floor for sorting (two summers). 1962 summer weekends,
Lazar's Restaurant, Centerport, L.I., bouncer; broken bottles and garbage
dumped out back. 1963 summer, Thomas Cook & Son banking dept., piles
of travelers checks; movie theatre usher, Boston (Roxbury); pile of unsorted
black marquee letters, a pile of popcorn lit up in a glass case. 1964 summer,
Bakery (factory), Boston, night-shift, loading trucks (an overturned pal-
ette of lemon meringue pies lying in a heap on the concrete floor.) 1965
summer Kennedy & Acker Construction, laborer, piles of sand, junk, scrap

lumber, etc. 1966-67 Peace Corps, Nigeria, survey & mapping (North-
ern Nigerian Gov. stipend for days spent in bush), abandoned mud huts
fallen into a heap, sacks of peanuts and sweet potato, cane stalks, graves,
dirt heaped over slaughtered Ibo. 1967 winter, Car transport, Istanbul
to Teheran, one-way trip; piles of snow and ice plowed into roadside
heaps. 1968 Bombay, movie extra (one day, ten rupees). 1968 Clam-
digger, Great South Bay, Long Island, a pile of clams in the flat-bottom
boat shoveled into bushel baskets. 1968 Cruise ship, *Franconia*, Cook's
Sales Rep, N.Y. to Bermuda, weekly trips, tiny heaps of caviar. 1968-69
WCBS-TV News, W 57th St. NYC, gofer assistant, then dispatch desk;
untended teletype machines, wire copy curling into a pile on the floor.
1969 Home builder, North Conway, New Hampshire, laborer; heaps of
stone, topsoil, stacks of railroad ties for steps and retaining walls. 1969?
Polling company, Harris? spring, conducted voter interviews in Man-
hattan. 1970-72 The Herald, weekly newspaper, NYC, foreign news
editor, then managing editor; heaps of unsold papers. 1972-74 The
Architectural Forum, managing editor. 1974—? Merchandising Week
major appliance Editor. 1974 (?) Ciardullo Architects, laborer (a few
weeks); pile of sand, pile of cement, shoveled & mixed in a metal bin, 3
to 1 ratio, add water as needed. 1974 Deliver telephone books, stacks of
them (a few days). 1975 Chainstore Age magazine, associate (?) editor.
1976-84 College of Financial Planning, test proctor, three Saturdays per
year; stacks of exam packets. 1977? Universal Limited Art Editions asst.
to Bucky Fuller, researcher, etc. per diem. 1977-87? Delivered Village
Voice off & on, 1 day per week; returns thrown into a heap in the back
of the van. 1980s freelance copy editor, writer, e.g., Franklin Mint Edi-
tions, word heaps. 1993-94 summers, Harvester machine operator, inva-
sive weed removal (milfoil), Lake Oscawanna, N.Y. (tranquil mornings
steering over the lake, submerged blades like a shark-toothed hedge-clip-
per, conveyor belt dumping a heap of clipped weeds into a cage, pull
alongside dock, back up a blue dump truck to the stern, dump the load of
weeds from boat onto truckbed, drive to woodlot a couple of miles away,
dump weeds onto a bigger heap from which rain would wash
seeds downhill to another lake).

ROSEBUSH IN FULL JUMBLED BLOOM

Rosebush in full jumbled bloom
Draped over the mailbox:
Who could resent such loveliness?

Only the mailman
Who yelps, curses and roars off again
In his stink-pot truck.

FRAGMENTS FROM MICHELANGELO AND ELSEWHERE

What greets me this morning, dove or owl, a coo or a hoot

*

She burns me, binds me, holds me, she's sugar to me

*

A sweet and cozy room in hell

*

Awake! You itchy, red-eyed, stertorous, half-naked, moon-lit sot

*

The future is scorched and my hands are cold

*

Steep road, brief joys, short day,
Another good habit lost along the way

*

Afloat in the same place, hour after hour
Desire and green shadows on the clear fast stream

*

It seemed an interesting idea at first, to carve my own tomb.
Mercy snuffed by a wild star.

*

I am made of absolutely nothing
Yet the sound of my breathing,
My wings shadow and frost

*

Hope ascends, a strand of smoke wrenching itself into a lily

*

Stonedust, chunks, chips flying, hammer and chisel calm my soul

*

With sugar, candles, a mule, a flask of sweet wine,
With no one to thank for these gifts
I am adrift in my lopsided boat